Governed by Magpies

Beatrice Holloway

TSL Drama

First published in Great Britain in 2018
By TSL Publications, Rickmansworth

Copyright © 2018 Beatrice Holloway

ISBN / 978-1-912416-18-9

Image courtesy of : https://pixabay.com/en/magpie-bird-feathers-wildlife-18968/

The right of Beatrice Holloway to be identified as the playwright/author of this work has been asserted by the author in accordance with the UK Copyright, Designs and Patents Act 1988.

All characters and events in this publication, other than those clearly in the public domain, are fictitious and any resemblance to actual persons, living or dead, is purely coincidental.

All rights reserved. No part of this publication may be reproduced, stored in a retrieval system or transmitted, in any form or by any means without the prior written permission of the publisher, nor be otherwise circulated in any form of binding or cover other than that in which it is published and without a similar condition being imposed on the subsequent buyer.

Rights of performance

Rights of performance for this play is controlled by TSL Publications (tslbooks.uk/Drama.) which issues a performing licence on payment of a fee and subject to a number of conditions (specified on tslbooks.uk/Drama.). This play is fully protected under the Copyright Laws of the British Commonwealth of Nations, the United States of America and all countries of the Berne and Universal Copyright Conventions. All rights, including stage, Motion Picture, Radio, Television, Public Reading and Translation into Foreign Languages are strictly reserved. It is an infringement of the Copyright to give any performance or public reading of this play before the fee has been paid and the licence issued. The Royalty Fee is subject to contract and subject to variation at the sole discretion of TSL Publications. In Territories Overseas the fees quoted may not apply. A fee will be quoted on application to TSL Publications.

Dedication

so many, alongside the performers,
to thank for such marvellous entertainment.

Governed by Magpies

Characters

STEWART	*similar age to Emma*
EMMA	*pregnant*
DR DAVID PETERSON	*older man*

Running Time

35-40 minutes

Setting

All action takes place in the kitchen.

One for sorrow
Two for joy.
Three for a kiss
And four for a boy.
Five for silver
Six for gold.
Seven a secret not to be told.

Scene 1

(*Lights up.*
EMMA *can be seen through the kitchen window hanging out washing in the garden.*)

EMMA: (*Faintly.*) One for sorrow, two for joy, three for a kiss and four for a boy, five for silver, six for gold seven a ...

STEWART: There you are. Thought I heard the machine stop.

EMMA: Yes, I want to get these bits of washing out. They could be dry before I meet mum and gran.

STEWART: You shouldn't be stretching like that. Can't be good for you or the baby can it? Don't want you rushing to hospital today do we?

EMMA: (*Sighs.*) All done. No, not really, especially as I've seen just one magpie this morning. You know what that means?

STEWART: (*Groans.*) Oh no! (*Pause.*) Come inside. It's freezing out there.

(*Sound of door being closed and movement about the kitchen. Indulgent laugh.*) Magpies! Just because our tree is full of them, you just can't let that old superstition go can you?

EMMA: (*Seriously.*) Don't Stew. Don't tempt fate. There might be something in it. You never know. You have to admit the old saying quite often proves right. My gran says ...

STEWART: (*Sceptical.*)Your gran's an old witch. She thrives on trying to frighten you.

EMMA: She's not! You stop that. She's a lovely old gran.

STEWART:	Okay. Okay, I know she loves you to bits, just like I do. But she does spout a load of old rubbish sometimes. Believe me. (*Pause.*) Can you put me up a few sarnies, while I make a flask of coffee?
EMMA:	You're not really going are you? If the tax man ...
STEWART:	(Sighing.) We need the money, Em. I already owe about three hundred on the card this month. The kid's due in a few weeks. I've got to get straight before then.

(*Kitchen noises – kettle etc.*)

EMMA:	But it isn't legit is it Stew? I don't want anything to happen to spoil the next few weeks – or ever come to that.
STEWART:	What's the problem? I'll be earning fair and square. If I do a good job they might tell their friends. House painting is hard graft believe me. Not many people like tackling their own place. They don't like the smell or getting themselves messed up. I should know.
EMMA:	(Sharply.) All the more reason to have a day off then.
STEWART:	I'm only thinking about the things the baby will need. You keep on about prams and cots and God knows what else. I 'm only doing my best.
EMMA:	But what if you're found out?
STEWART:	Who's going to tell? Who's going know, for God's sake?
EMMA:	It isn't that Stew. (*Pause.*) I just think with your record ...
STEWART:	(*Raising his voice.*) Trust you! Trust you to throw that up. All that happened when I was fifteen, sixteen? You know that. All boys' stuff. My slate's clean. I've been straight for five years and more, so let it rest will you?

EMMA:	(*Tearfully.*) You know you were caught when you tried to break into that house in Bramble Lane. That was a close thing. You could have been sent to prison for that. My dad says the police always pick on people known to them first.
STEWART:	(*Exasperated.*) For God's sake Em! Give it a rest. I'm not a criminal. I was a juvenile delinquent. That's how the newspapers rated me.
EMMA:	Yes, but ...
STEWART:	(*Snaps at her.*) A couple of times joy-riding and ONE shoplifting offence! Hardly earth shattering is it!
EMMA:	AND attempted burglary.
STEWART:	Are you going to make them sandwiches or what? (*Pause.*) And by the way. I reckon your dad would have a field day if I did go off the rails. I can hear him now. 'That boy ...'
EMMA:	Don't start on about my family again. They think the world of you, including my dad. They've helped us a lot – getting this place sorted for a start.(*Pause.*)
STEWART:	Em. I only want ...
EMMA:	(*Tearfully.*) I'm really proud of you Stew. but I do worry about you. What if you went inside? How would I cope? And not only that, you'd find it hard getting a job when you got out. I think about these sort of things all the time.
STEWART:	Now you're being daft. I'm not doing anything thousands of other blokes don't do. Just trying to make ends meet, and keep their family together.
EMMA:	(*Desperately.*) I can't help it. I saw that magpie! Just one this morning. You know, one for sorrow ...

STEWART: Jeez Em! I didn't ask you to get pregnant did I? If only it hadn't happened so soon. We agreed to wait two years and get a decent place together. I'd hardly started decorating the place, then (*Sarcastically*) but oh no! You ...

EMMA: It takes two you know.

(*A long silence.*)

STEWART: (*Softened tone.*) Come here love. Give us a cuddle. I know it takes two and well, you're irresistible.

EMMA: What! Even with this bump in front, you still think I'm irresistible?

STEWART: (*Softly.*) I love you Emma Mason, even with your bump.

EMMA: Our bump.

STEWART: Listen Em. I want this baby to have everything that we can possibly give it, so we do need a bit extra. You see that don't you? (*Pause.*) Tell you what. I'll make this my last cash in hand job. How's that? (*Pause.*) I'll see if there's any overtime going at work. Let's see how it pans out, okay?

EMMA: (*Brightly.*) You mean it? Really? That would be better than anything. I'll help all can. I'll go back to work as soon as the baby can be left. Mum said she'd help out.

STEWART: We'll see. I don't want my child stuffed with her nonsense as well.

EMMA: Let's cross that bridge when we get there, okay? Now, did you say you wanted some sandwiches? I'll do them right away. Cheese alright with a bit of pickle?

STEWART: Yeah. Right. (*They kiss.*) I'll get the bike out. Back in a minute.

(**EMMA** *hums happily as she bustles about.* **STEWART** *returns.*)

STEWART: Right, I'm off. You know where to get me if ... (*Significant pause.*) you know, if anything happens. I'm at Woodend Drive. I've written the number down on that envelope by the phone. If anything starts, let me know straight away. I want to be there. See you about six I should think.

EMMA: Shall I walk to the gate with you?

STEWART: No, you stay in the warm. I hope to be home before it gets dark. (*Adds cheekily.*) Don't want to be picked up for no lights do I? Might add to my criminal record.

EMMA: (*Slaps him lightly.*) Oh! You ...

STEWART: Ouch! Now listen. If you're seeing your mum and gran this afternoon, don't go listening to any more of their old wives' tales. Hear me?

EMMA: I don't.

STEWART: You do. I bet when you were a kid, you never trod on cracks on the pavement did you?

EMMA: Alright, I admit they do go on a bit. But they are so excited. The first grandchild and great grandchild. You can't blame them really.

STEWART: Heaven help us when it arrives then.

EMMA: Yes, I know. We'll have to watch they don't spoil baby. Well, not too much. One week it's a girl because it's lying so so and then the next week they spot something different and swear it's a boy (*Excitedly.*) Look Stew, two magpies – two for joy.

STEWART: (*In a mock warning voice.*) Emma.

EMMA: Oh! Go on with you. It's only a bit of fun, but you have to admit ...

STEWART: (*Kisses her.*) I'm not admitting anything! Cheers then. See you later. Have fun in your witches' coven. 'Double, double, toil and trouble – argh! – and take it easy will you.

(*Bicycle bell rings as he rides off.*)

EMMA: (*Laughing and shouting after him.*) At six I'll brew up something special just for you.

Scene 2

(*Later a clock chimes six.*
EMMA *is working in the kitchen.*)

STEWART: Anyone home? Where's my girl? Something smells good. Is that the witches' brew I was promised?

EMMA: (*Proudly.*) Lamb stew actually. Mum told me …

STEWART: (*Entering kitchen and teasing.*) I warned you.

EMMA: All I was going to say, (*Exchange of kisses.*) there must be three magpies somewhere – all I was going to say was, Mum told me how to make dumplings. I've just put them in and dinner will be ready in about half and hour.

STEWART: Good, That gives us some time because I've got something to show you. (*Pause.*) Look what I've found.

EMMA: (*Slowly.*) Very expensive briefcase (*Pause.*) especially with gold letters on. D.P. Been run over a couple of times by the look of things.

STEWART: I found it in the gutter, papers everywhere. I picked them up. Someone will be glad to have them back I shouldn't wonder. (*Teasing slyly.*) I reckon six magpies must have crossed my path today.

EMMA: What do you mean?

STEWART: I mean that there's someone out there who'll be glad to get them back. Six magpies for gold isn't it?

EMMA:	(*Papers rustle. Agitated.*) Stew. They're government papers. I'm sure of it. Look, it says 'Private and Confidential'. (*Pause. And more paper rustling.*)
STEWART:	So?
EMMA:	(*Shocked.*) Stewart, this one's marked 'Top Secret'. Put them away. Take them to the police station. They'll only bring us trouble.
STEWART:	Hang on a minute. Let's have a good look first.
EMMA:	I don't like it Stew. They could bring us real trouble.
STEWART:	Like what?
EMMA:	I don't know. I've just got a feeling about it.
STEWART:	(*Very excited. Pause.*) What have we got here? Very interesting! Something very private. Personal letters by the look of things.
EMMA:	Personal letters?
STEWART:	(*Softly chuckling.*) You bet your sweet life on it. Personal and hot my girl!
EMMA:	(*Sharply.*) Well, you've no business reading them. Put them away. They're private, not for you to see. How would you like someone going through your stuff?
STEWART:	I've got nothing to hide, not like this fellow.
EMMA:	That's not the point Stew.
STEWART:	Listen Em. What if I tell you they belong to a certain Sir Peterson, and what if I tell you he is a married man and these letters are from someone called – Bob?
EMMA:	Stewart! Don't be so nasty-minded! Put that case way now. Take it to the police first thing tomorrow.

STEWART:	Don't you see Em. He'd probably be glad to have these back safely. (*Paper rustles*.) Listen. 'My dearest darling David. How can I begin to explain the effect that being close to you has on me? You were so gentle last ...'
EMMA:	(*Distressed.*) Stop! I don't want to hear. Please, (*Pause.*) Put them away.
STEWART:	No? Well let me tell you. (*Emphasises.*) We need the money. How do you think this Sir Peter will feel if this stuff got into the papers?
EMMA:	If you ever do a thing like that Stewart Mason, I'd never forgive you.
STEWART:	(*Mock innocence.*) What did I say? I only said 'if'. (*Thoughtfully.*) No. I reckon a more personal approach would be better. (*Briskly.*) There must be an address somewhere. Should be among this little lot.
EMMA:	(*Nearly hysterical.*) Can you hear yourself? Do you know what you're saying?
STEWART:	(*Surprised.*) What? (*Pause.*) What?
EMMA:	(*Pause. Then dramatically*.) Blackmail.
STEWART:	(*Heatedly.*) No it's not. I'd be doing the bloke a favour.
EMMA:	It is blackmail Stewart. You know that. And it's evil, wicked. You'll be sorry, believe me. He'll go to the police. (*Pause.*) What's the date on them anyway?
STEWART:	Mostly around ...
EMMA:	Ages ago. And THAT sort of thing isn't so, so – well it's accepted better today.
STEWART:	Nobody likes skeletons in the cupboard. The press would have a field day with this little lot. (*Pause.*) Look, we need the money Em.
EMMA:	Not this way.

STEWART: Listen carefully will you. I'm so desperate that I've been close to burglary a couple of times on my way home these dark nights.

EMMA: Stewart!

STEWART: Well, bloody idiots leaving windows open they're asking for it.

EMMA: Stewart. Don't ever let me hear you say that again. I keep telling you, we'll manage. We've got each other now. (*Softly*.) But not for long if you do something stupid.

STEWART: (*Resignedly*.) But I didn't, did I? Believe me, it'd be easy. Dark nights and a bicycle get away. No trouble at all.

EMMA: So that's what you've been brooding about. I thought there was something up when you kept chewing your fingernails. You always do that. That's when I know you're planning something.

STEWART: Yes Em. I'm brooding alright.

(*Pause*.)

EMMA: Take the papers to the police in the morning Stew. Please. Perhaps there'll be a reward, you never know. If there is that way you can spend it with a clear conscience.

STEWART: I'll think about it.

EMMA: You'll bring more worry for both of us if you don't. I'm warning you. (*Sighs*.) Well, dinner is just about ready. Have a wash while I dish up.

STEWART: (*Beginning to read another letter*.) 'Dearest, I find it harder and harder to keep our wonderful secret. When are we going to let the cat out of the bag. So many people are going to be surprised. I suppose we must wait until everyone is back from their holidays. Together for life! Wonderful isn't it. I do, do love you so much. especially, well you know when! Call me soon ...

EMMA: Ready?

STEWART: (*Thinking aloud.*) I'll read more when Em goes to bed. She's terrified something awful will happen. These other papers ... all seem to be marked 'Top Secret' or 'Confidential'. She's right of course. Me in prison and a new baby, she'd never manage. Suppose I'd better do what she wants. Keep the peace. Don't fancy doing time anyway. (*Brightening up.*) The cops will be blown away when they see me walk in tomorrow.

(*To Emma.*) Right love, let's have it. I'm starving.

EMMA: Like it?

STEWART: Smashing.

EMMA: (*Flatly.*) Mums are good for some things then?

STEWART: Come on Em. Cheer up. You're right as usual. What's it like being right all the time? Don't worry, I'll go first thing in the morning. Okay? (*Sighs.*) Keeping them will probably do more harm than good as you say.

Scene 3

(*Next day. Telephone ringing in kitchen.*)

SIR DAVID: Is that Mr Mason? This is David Peterson here. The police were kind enough to give me your name after you handed in my briefcase this morning.

STEWART: (*Surprised.*) Er. Yeah, this is Stewart Mason.

SIR DAVID: I wonder? Would it be convenient if I called round? About those papers you see. I feel I owe you an explanation. Could we have a chat. Today if possible?

STEWART: Yeah, sure.

SIR DAVID: About seven thirty suit you?

STEWART: Perfect. That'll be fine. We'll have finished our dinner by then.

SIR DAVID: (*Briskly.*) Right. I'll see you then. It's number sixty one, Meadow Walk, I believe.

STEWART: Yes, you can't miss us. Got a huge oak in the front. Always full of magpies!

SIR DAVID: Goodbye for now. Look forward to meeting you later.

(*Doorbell rings.*)

EMMA: (*Flustered.*) That's him! Mind now Stewart, be careful. Don't make any trouble. (*Pause.*) Go on then, answer the door.

STEWART: Come on in sir. This is my wife, Emma. Can we get you a cup of something? Erm …

SIR DAVID: No, no, I'm fine thanks. May I sit down?

EMMA: Yes, of course. Please do.

SIR DAVID: Well now. I daresay you had quite a shock finding my briefcase. I understand from the police that you also picked up the papers that got scattered around.

STEWART: Yes, didn't take long though.

SIR DAVID: I'm very glad you did young man. Nothing at all seems to be missing. (*Pause.*) Such a relief I can tell you.

EMMA: There Stewart. I told you he'd be worried sick.

SIR DAVID: To be honest, I hadn't missed them until the police called. Put them on top of the car yesterday while I unlocked the door, then drove off and forgot all about it. Damn silly thing to do.

STEWART: I thought it might be something like that. Happens quite often according to the Insurance people.

SIR DAVID: Yes, but I should have been a great deal more careful. Government papers, very hush hush, if you see what I mean. (*Pause.*) I lost my wife you see.

EMMA: What? Lost her somewhere or ...

SIR DAVID: That's right. She died a couple of months ago. It's been on my mind. Lost concentration. Not at all acceptable in my position. Not acceptable at all.

STEWART: But quite understandable in the circumstances, I'd say. I'd be devastated to lose Em ...

SIR DAVID: Since her death I've made a number of little mistakes. Nothing as terrible as this latest. Misplacing government papers. My God. I must have been in a state for a long while. I suspect my friends and colleagues must have been covering for me all the while, but there's no way they would be able to bail me out of this spot of bother.

STEWART:	The papers are that serious then?
SIR DAVID:	Yes, very much so.
EMMA:	I kept saying to Stew. He must take them to the police, didn't I Stew?
STEWART:	Yeah, yes.
SIR DAVID:	Well I can't thank you both enough. You've really saved, well I suppose, my career and reputation.
STEWART:	I started to put them in number order, but there were so many, I'm afraid I gave up. (*Laughs.*) Anyway, Em called me for dinner and I was starving. But if they're all there, then that's all that really matters isn't it?
SIR DAVID:	Thanks to you yes, but ... (*Hesitates.*) I do have to ask ... State Secrets Act you know. (*Pause.*) I do have to ask if by any chance you actually read any of the documents? Have you spoken to anyone about what you read?
STEWART:	No, I can't say I actually read them.
SIR DAVID:	Good, good.
STEWART:	No, to be honest, I did start to read them. I mean, well, if you saw something marked 'Secret' and 'Confidential' wouldn't you be tempted?
SIR DAVID:	Mmm. Maybe, maybe. But ...
STEWART:	But to be truthful I found them all a bit boring. Know what I mean? And I couldn't understand most of it except words like nuclear fallout, civilian casualties, warheads – things like that.
SIR DAVID:	But you definitely haven't spoken to anybody about this, have you?
EMMA:	(*Nervously.*) No, no. We haven't seen anyone today, have we Stew?
SIR DAVID:	(*Sighs with relief.*) I'm pleased about that. Saves such a lot of hassle, paperwork and such like you understand.

STEWART:	You mean, we could be investigated or something?
SIR DAVID:	Yes, something like that.
STEWART:	No thanks! We want a quiet life, don't we Em. No M.F.I. or suchlike here thank you very much.
SIR DAVID:	Yes, quite. (*Pause.*) I think it would be in both our interests to keep quiet about all of this. I too would be in great deal of trouble. Probably crucified by the Press as well as the Government.
STEWART:	(*Tentatively.*) The letters?
SIR DAVID:	Ah yes, the letters.
STEWART:	I have to confess I did read some of those.
EMMA:	(*Apprehensively.*) Stewart.
SIR DAVID:	Lovely aren't they?
STEWART:	(*Carefully.*) We, er I, we know about that sort of thing really but ...
EMMA:	Oh Stewart. Don't say ...
STEWART:	It's alright Em. Sir David knows what I mean.
SIR DAVID:	(*Laughs heartily.*) Bob would enjoy what you're thinking, young man. (*Laughs again.*) Yes, would laugh out loud.
STEWART:	(*Defensively.*) A long time ago, and all that, but even today people might think ...
EMMA:	(*Almost in tears.*) Stewart! You promised.
SIR DAVID:	Don't upset yourself my dear. Bob was like that. Loved to shock people into believing the unbelievable. I went along with it of course, Anything to please the lady.
	(**EMMA** and **STEWART** *gasp in amazement together.*)
SIR DAVID:	Yes, married the little madam over thirty years ago. My wife, you know. Real name Roberta, but called herself Bob or Bobby. Loved her, always

	have, always will. (*Pause. Emotionally.*) Miss her, miss her dreadfully. (*Long pause.*)
EMMA:	(*Softly.*) I'm so glad we were able to get the letters back to you. They must be your most important memories of her.
SIR DAVID:	Couldn't have put it better myself young lady. (*Pause.*) I see you're near to adding to your family. We had three children you know. Two girls and a boy. Left home now of course. Got families of their own.
EMMA:	Yes, just about three weeks to go.
SIR DAVID:	So what are you hoping for? A boy? A girl?
EMMA:	(*Laughing.*) Oh it's sure to be a boy. I saw four magpies earlier. That's always a good sign.
SIR DAVID:	Four magpies eh!
STEWART:	(*Quiet cough.*) You'll have to excuse her, Sir David. Sensitive time for her you understand, pregnant and all that.
SIR DAVID:	Quite! Understand perfectly.
STEWART:	Em is governed by magpies at the moment. The rhyme you know, One for sorrow – how does it go Em?
EMMA:	Oh Stewart! You know that's not true! Things just happen by coincidence and then I see the right number of magpies.
STEWART:	Well you would, wouldn't you! We've got a whole flock of them in the front garden. Not only that, her family are full of weird superstitions. I tell you I have to be on my toes or else I'd get dragged in.
SIR DAVID:	(*Laughs.*) I think I know exactly what you mean. Bobby's favourite saying when she saw an ambulance went something like. 'Hold your collar, nev-

	er swallow, 'til you've seen a dog.' What the connection was I never found out! (*All laugh.*)
EMMA:	I don't know that one. My nan might. She knows hundreds. She says crossed knives are unlucky, so is putting new shoes on the table and spilling salt.
STEWART:	For goodness sake Em give it a rest They are only superstitions and silly ones at that.
SIR DAVID:	A lot of them have quite interesting foundations I believe, but nowadays science seems to have an explanation for everything. (*Pause.*) I think it's time I was leaving you good folk.
STEWART:	You're more than welcome to stay a while. Let me get you a drink of something. We usually have a cup of tea around this time.
SIR DAVID:	No. Thanks all the same. I'll be on my way.
EMMA:	It's been lovely meeting you Sir David. I'm so glad Stew took the papers in to the police. I couldn't bear it if Stewart got into any sort of trouble right now.
SIR DAVID:	Trouble? No, no, he did the right thing. Though I do believe he quite enjoyed my letters. (*Laughs.*) A bit naughty of him wouldn't you say?
EMMA:	Yes, and I told him so in no uncertain terms!
STEWART:	Are you two ganging up on me? (*All laugh.*) I'll see you out Sir David.
SIR DAVID:	Before I go, let me say once again how much I appreciate your honesty and discretion. This really was a very sensitive issue you know.
STEWART:	Glad it's all worked out.
SIR DAVID:	I hope you won't be offended, but, well I don't want to embarrass you with a reward as such. (*Pause.*) But would you ahem accept this er

EMMA: (*Overcome.*) We couldn't ...

STEWART: (*Quickly interrupting.*) What Emma means is we can't thank you enough for your gift.

SIR DAVID: I thought perhaps it would be useful especially for what a new baby needs nowadays. Stretchy things for them to grow into Bob always said. That right Emma?

STEWART: Em? Say something.

EMMA: Yes, and thank you, Thank you so much. There are some more things I need and I can get something really special for him as well.

STEWART: This is really very generous of you. We're delighted.

SIR DAVID: There's just one other thing before I really get on my way. Remind me Emma, how that magpie rhyme goes again will you?

STEWART: (*Laughs.*) You may be sorry!

SIR DAVID: Go ahead Emma. Let's see if I remember it.

EMMA: One for sorrow, two for joy, three for a kiss and four for a boy. Five for silver, six for gold and ...

SIR DAVID: Seven a secret never to be told. Yes, I remember it now.

STEWART: Oh no! Not another convert.

SIR DAVID: I think young man, you'd better take note of the rhyme yourself. As Emma said, quite often the situation seems to correspond to the ditty and I would say that number seven is the one you should pay most attention too.

STEWART: What's number seven Em?

EMMA: Seven a secret never to be told.

STEWART:	Ah! Got you. I understand. Trust me Sir David, magpies or no magpies, all of the secrets will be safe with me.
SIR DAVID:	Good. We'll say no more. Now I really must be off. Good evening to you both, and good luck with the offspring.
STEWART:	Good evening, and thanks again.
EMMA:	Yes, thank you. Thank you so much (SIR DAVID *leaves*. *Pause*.)
EMMA:	Oh Stewart, I was so right wasn't I?
STEWART:	I'll say! Look! Two hundred pounds and with what I got yesterday, we're a few quids in. You can have that sprog anytime you like now!

(*Relieved laughing and cuddles.*
Lights down.)

THE END

Plays by Beatrice

A Certain Monday

Connie's Lovely Boy

From Commoner to Coronet

Governed by Magpies

In Less than 10 Minutes

Short Plays for Young Actors

About Beatrice

Beatrice Holloway is a playwright and author who has been writing children's stories since 2014. In 2015, Beatrice was appointed Children's Storyteller on Hillingdon Narrowboats Association which has led her to write about canal life. TSL has published Beatrice's stories about Rhys and his friends. You can contact Beatrice through her author-site or Facebook.

Beatrice has written a number of children's books: *Towing Path Tales*, *More Towing Path Tales* and *A Particular Year* as well as a number of science experiments for children – all available as ebooks.

The London Borough of Hillingdon library service has published two of her children's stories and awarded her with a Certificate of merit – 'In recognition of an outstanding contribution to the Arts'. Beatrice was also awarded a Lottery Grant to write a commissioned historical play: *Commoner to Coronet*.

She also has two adult books, *A man from the North East* (reprinted by TSL) and *Elusive Destiny*, and she is currently working on a third novel, *Archie's Children*.

Beatrice is a retired teacher and a member of The Society of Women Writers and Journalists and the Society of Authors.

www.ingramcontent.com/pod-product-compliance
Lightning Source LLC
Chambersburg PA
CBHW071804040426
42446CB00012B/2711